MATERIALS THAT MATTER

WOOD

Neil Morris

amicus

Published by Amicus
P.O. Box 1329
Mankato, MN 56002

Printed in the United States of America,
at Corporate Graphics, North Mankato, Minnesota.

Library of Congress Cataloging-in-Publication Data
Morris, Neil, 1946-
 Wood / by Neil Morris.
    p. cm. -- (Materials that matter)
 Summary: "Discusses wood as a material, including historical uses, current uses, collection, and recycling"--Provided by publisher.
 Includes index.
 ISBN 978-1-60753-070-1 (lib. bdg.)
 1. Wood--Juvenile literature. I. Title.
 TA419.M66 2011
 634.9'8--dc22

                                                                    2010001621

Created by Appleseed Editions, Ltd.
Designed by Helen James
Edited by Mary-Jane Wilkins
Artwork by Graham Rosewarne
Picture research by Su Alexander

Photograph acknowledgements
page 4 Henry Westheim Photography/Alamy; 6 North Wind Picture Archives/Alamy; 7 Travelpixs/Alamy; 8 Bibliotheque de l'Arsenal Paris/Kharbine-Tapabor/Coll.Jean Vigne/The Art Archive; 9 David Kilpatrick/Alamy; 10 Chris Luneski/Alamy; 11 & 12 Gunter Marx/Alamy; 14 Neil McAllister/Alamy; 15 Nordicphotos/Alamy; 16 H Mark Weidman Photography/Alamy; 17 J Baylor Robots/NGS Image Collection/The Art Archive; 18 James Hawkins/Alamy; 19 John James/Alamy; 20 Susan Yates/Alamy; 22 Tibor Bognar/Alamy; 23 Jeff Morgan Industry And Work/Alamy; 25 Photoshot Holdings Ltd/Alamy; 26 Julio Etchart/Alamy; 27 Robert Harding Picture Library/Alamy; 28 Andrew N Gagg/Alamy; 29 Dennis Kunkel Microscopy Inc./Phototake/Alamy
Front cover Christine Osborne Pictures/Alamy

DAD0041
32010

9 8 7 6 5 4 3 2 1

Contents

What Is Wood?

You can probably think of lots of things that are made of wood. Your desk or table may be wooden. The pencil you write with may be made of wood, too. There are many different kinds of wood; some are very heavy while others are quite light. But they all come from the same source—trees.

*Wood comes in many shades of color. It also has different **grain** (see page 15). You can see grain lines at the ends of these boards.*

Part of a Tree

Wood makes up the trunk and branches of trees. It is the main substance in all woody plants. Scientists call it plant tissue, or **xylem** (from the Greek word for wood). Trees use this tissue to carry water and minerals up from their roots.

When the liquid reaches a tree's leaves, it is combined with sunlight and **carbon dioxide** gas from the air. This process, called **photosynthesis**, helps plants make their own sugary food (called sap). Liquid travels through the tiny cells that make up wood.

Using Wood Again

Wood from buildings or furniture can be recycled when the original item is no longer needed (see pages 26–27 on recycling). The wood can be reused as it is, or it can be sawed up or ground down into wood chips.

Recycling helps the environment in many ways. If we recycle wood, we need to cut down fewer trees. We also use less energy than when we fell, saw, and prepare new timber. This reduces **pollution** and the amount of waste we dump in landfills.

These cells are shaped like narrow, hollow tubes. There may be as many as 380 billion cells in one cubic yard (500 billion cells per m³) of wood. The cells can also store sap for future use.

Tiny Fibers

The walls of wood cells are made mainly of a soft substance called **cellulose**. This word comes from the French *cellule*, meaning small cell. The tiny, threadlike fibers that make up cellulose are only 0.004 inch (0.1 mm) wide and just over 0.04 inch (1 mm) long.

Cellulose makes up about half of the weight of wood. Another natural substance, called **lignin**, binds the tiny fibers together.

Inside a Tree Trunk

When a tree is cut down, we can see two kinds of wood inside the trunk. Near the center is a darker, drier section of **heartwood**. This is older wood that is dead but still helps support the tree. The living cells of lighter, softer **sapwood** surround the heartwood. A layer of bark covers the outside of the trunk.

Trees make a new layer of wood every year. The layers form growth rings, which tell us how old a tree was when it was felled. How old was this tree?

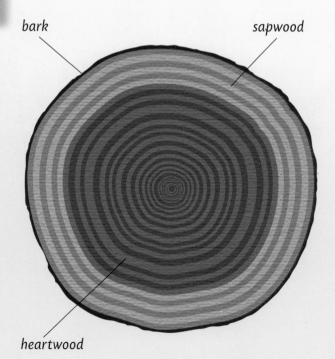

bark

sapwood

heartwood

Fire, Shelter, and Ships

There have been trees on Earth for hundreds of millions of years. The earliest human probably used fallen branches to dig for roots and other food, as well as to knock down fruits and nuts. Their descendants made tools and built shelters from wood. They also used it for making fire.

The Discovery of Fire

Historians believe that humans first used wood to make controlled fires more than 500,000 years ago. **Prehistoric** humans may have seen lightning strike trees and set fire to them. This gave them the idea of lighting wood by making sparks. They made the sparks by rubbing sticks together or striking pieces of **flint**. Fire made a huge difference to people's lives. They used it to cook meat, which was then much easier and safer to eat. Fire provided warmth and light in caves and other shelters, as well as frightening away wild animals. The heat from fire was also useful for hardening stone and wooden tools.

This nineteenth-century picture shows prehistoric humans making a fire.

Homes and Hunting

Around 400,000 years ago, humans in Europe were using wood in new ways. At the site of Terra Amata in southern France, prehistoric people built oval-shaped wooden huts. They used strong branches to make these shelters. At around the same time, hunters at Schöningen in Germany were using sharp stone tools to cut 6.5-foot (2 m) long spears from spruce trees. The spears had sharp points, and hunters threw them like javelins to kill wild animals.

Early Ships

The earliest boats were dugout canoes, which people hollowed out from tree trunks. The ancient Egyptians built boats from planks of wood nearly 5,000 years ago. They found that the strongest planks came from the **cedar** trees, which grew

This boat was found beside the Great Pyramid at Giza in Egypt. The boat is at least 4,500 years old and was rebuilt from 1,200 pieces of cedar wood.

in Lebanon. The ancient Greeks and Romans built larger wooden ships, both war **galleys** and merchant vessels. An ordinary Roman trading ship could carry hundreds of tons (t) of grain from Egypt.

Wooden Tools

The first farmers used digging sticks and other wooden tools to help them plant crops. The wooden **plow** was invented about 8,000 years ago and used to turn over the soil before farmers planted seeds. Later, iron was added to the plow blade, to make it stronger.

ROMAN PLANTING

Today we call wood a renewable resource, because new trees can be planted to replace those we chop down. The ancient Romans also planted trees and brought seedlings to the Italian peninsula from all around their empire, including Lebanon. They planted groves of trees, which gave them a constant supply of wood.

Looking after Forests

Wood is a valuable material because it has so many uses. In prehistoric times, there were plenty of trees in most parts of the world. But when people started farming, they made great gaps in the forests. They did this by harvesting wood and cutting down trees to make room for their crops, houses, and animals.

As settlements and villages grew into towns and cities, people chopped down more trees, and forests grew smaller. People living in towns needed wood for houses and furniture. Looking after the source of wood—trees—became important everywhere.

Oaks for Shipbuilding

During the Middle Ages in Europe, countries were using more and more wood to build ships. Britain, France, Portugal, and Spain all built large navies. Their fleets of ships were for both trade and war. In England, King Henry VII (reigned 1485–1509) founded a dockyard at Portsmouth, where woodworkers built large cargo vessels. His son Henry VIII (reigned 1509–47) opened another dock on the River Thames, which built warships. Shipbuilders needed more than 2,000 large oak trees

A fifteenth-century French painting showing carpenters at work. The artist imagined that this was how Noah's ark was built.

to make one of these ships. At this time, adventurous sailors were setting off around the world on voyages of discovery. They all traveled in wooden ships.

Heating and Cooking

Many people lived in timber-framed houses during the Middle Ages. In winter, they burned huge amounts of wood to heat their homes and cook meals. By the seventeenth century, they were also burning large quantities of **charcoal**.

People made charcoal by heating wood in an enclosed space without air. This might be an oven or a pile of wood covered with **sod** or soil. Charcoal burned slowly and gave off great heat. During the eighteenth century, miners dug up great quantities of coal, but it was smoky and sooty when it burned. They wanted to go on burning wood or charcoal, but this meant cutting down more trees.

Forest Law

The process of cutting down trees and destroying forests is called **deforestation**. A document dating back to 1538 mentions deforesting and shows that even in those days people were aware of the problem.

RESTORE RESTORE RESTORE RESTORE

RENEWING A VALUABLE RESOURCE

Today, environmentalists stress the importance of renewable resources. By this they mean materials and sources of energy that do not run out when they are used, such as geothermal, solar, water, and wind power. They also mean wood, which is used but can be replaced by planting new trees. Good forest management makes this possible.

Kings and noblemen owned many forests, which they used for harvesting wood and hunting animals (for food and sport). Laws protecting forests were especially strong in France and Germany, where schools of forestry sprang up during the nineteenth century. Foresters realized that they had to manage woodland, and they planted new trees to replace those they cut down.

The Berber people of North Africa use a traditional earth oven for cooking. They burn wood and charcoal inside the oven.

Felling Trees for Logs

The job of felling trees and turning them into logs of wood is called logging. Loggers trim the felled trees to remove twigs and leaves, then transport the logs to a sawmill. There, saws cut the logs into boards or planks (see pages 12–13). Foresters have to choose very carefully where they allow logging companies to fell trees.

Today, most planted forests contain mainly **softwood** trees, and they are often made up of just one kind of tree. Older forests may have many different kinds of **hardwood** trees, which usually take longer to grow.

Clearing or Selecting

When loggers clear an area of forest, they chop down all the trees but leave some branches and small pieces of wood from the felling to enrich the soil for new seedlings. Foresters then replant the area. Alternatively, loggers may select and cut down a number of older trees and leave the younger trees for future years.

Chopping and Sawing

Years ago, woodcutters chopped down trees with axes. Today, lumberjacks mostly use motor-driven chain saws to cut through the thick trunks. The saw's chain has a sharp cutting tooth on each link, and the chain moves around very fast. The tree feller cuts a wedge-shaped notch, or undercut, on the side of the trunk facing the direction in which he wants the tree to fall. Cutting this notch takes some skill, and it makes sure that a felled tree causes as little damage as possible to other trees and the workers.

A logger uses his chain saw to fell a tree in Oregon.

A tugboat tows a barge full of logs to a sawmill on the Fraser River in British Columbia, Canada.

Dragging and Driving

Loggers may cut the trees into smaller lengths before they take them away.

This depends on the size of the trees, what kind of wood they produce, and what the wood will be used for. Loggers use cranes or other machines to drag the logs to a clearing, where they are loaded onto trucks or train cars. These take the logs to the nearest sawmill.

HARDWOOD AND SOFTWOOD

Hardwood comes from broad-leaved trees, such as birch, elm, or oak. Most hardwood trees are **deciduous**, which means they drop their leaves in autumn. Softwood comes from needle-leaved trees, such as cedar, fir, or pine. Most softwood trees are **evergreen**, which means they keep their leaves all year round. Most softwood trees are also conifers, which means they grow their seeds in cones.

World's Top Loggers

Six countries together produce nearly half the world's wood.

Country	Billion board feet	Million cubic meters
USA	188	444
India	140	330
China	125	294
Brazil	104	245
Russia	88	207
Canada	83	196

Source: Food and Agriculture Organization, 2007

At the Sawmill

The sawmill has large, power-driven saws, which cut logs into boards and planks. Centuries ago, water power drove the saws. Today, most are driven by electricity or natural gas, and many provide their own power by burning waste wood. The sawmills keep down the amount of waste wood they create by using computers to determine the best way to cut the wood.

Cutting and Sawing

First mechanical cutters take the bark off the logs. A conveyor chain then carries the logs to the head saw, which cuts the log into a chosen pattern. Computers determine the best pattern and guide the saw as the log moves back and forth. Next, band saws and circular saws cut the blocks of wood into different-sized boards and planks.

Some of these are sliced again into thinner boards. These go through more saws, called edgers and thinners, which cut them into standard lengths and widths.

This mobile sawmill in a small community in northern Canada uses a steel circular saw to cut logs to size.

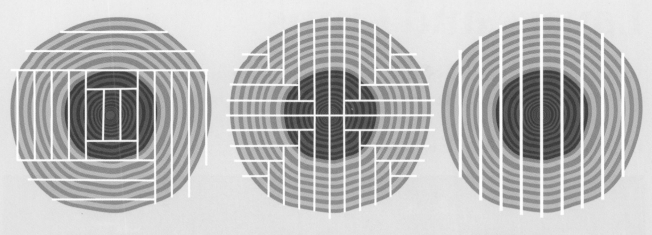

Plain-sawn   Quartersawn   Through-and-through

These three different sawing patterns show how shapes of wood are created at the first cut.

Sorting and Seasoning

Workers called graders check and sort the sawn timber. They grade the wood according to how good it is and watch for **defects**. Different grades of wood are used for various purposes, such as flooring or furniture. At this stage, the wood contains a lot of moisture and is called **greenwood**. Next it is seasoned, or dried, to prevent it from warping and splitting. The easiest way to do this is by drying the wood in the open air. A quicker method is kiln drying, when the wood is heated in an oven by warm moving air. This can take hours rather than the weeks it takes to air dry wood.

Largest Sawmill

The world's largest sawmill is the Canadian Canfor Corporation's mill in Houston, British Columbia. It saws about 600 million board feet (830,000 m³) of softwood a year. An adjacent facility converts the sawmill's waste sawdust and shavings into wood pellets to be used as **biomass fuel** (see page 19).

Using Up Waste

Sawmills create a lot of waste sawdust and wood particles. Years ago, workers burned this waste in large ovens to get rid of it. This made a lot of smoke and polluted the air. Today, the waste is used in many different ways. Some is burned to produce energy (see page 19). Some is used to make **fiberboard** (see page 15). Some larger pieces are broken down into wood chips and become a **raw material** for making paper (see page 16). Bark is used in the same way, and some is used to cover or improve soil in gardens.

RECYCLE RECYCLE RECYCLE RECYCLE

Layers and Chips

We usually think of wood as a solid block of material. This is wood straight from the tree, which has been cut or sawn into pieces. But most tree trunks are not big enough to produce wide boards or planks.

Gluing Layers Together

We can glue separate boards together, say, to make a tabletop. If this is done well, you can hardly see the joins between the boards. There are many kinds of **engineered wood**, which joins smaller pieces together.

Plywood is made from thin sheets of wood, called plies or **veneers**. A machine slices the sheets from a log or thick board as it moves past a fixed knife.

Workers sort thin plies (or veneers) in a plywood factory in India.

Glued together, the veneers make strong plywood. Manufacturers use an odd number of veneers, three for three-ply wood, five for five-ply, and so on. The grain direction of each veneer is at right angles to the next. This adds strength and stops the plywood from warping.

RECYCLE RECYCLE RECYCLE RECYCLE

REUSING CHIPS

Small pieces of wood from sawmills are made into particleboard. This is a good form of recycling. Some particleboard has a veneer glued to its surface—this is called lamination.

WOOD GRAIN

Have you noticed that most pieces of wood have a streaky pattern? This is called the grain, and it flows in one direction. It comes from the way in which wood fibers join together to form lines. The grain often makes a piece of wood look attractive, and every grain pattern is unique. The grain is important in engineered woods, and you can sometimes see where pieces of wood have been stuck together because of the different grain patterns.

Blockboard is made from strips of softwood layered like a sandwich. The two outer layers are thin sheets of hardwood veneer. The filling between the two layers is made of solid strips of softwood. The sandwich is glued together under high pressure.

Pressing Fibers into Sheets

To make fiberboard, a machine presses wood fibers, such as sawdust or tiny wood chips, tightly together and then mixes them with chemicals and **resins**. Fiberboard sheets are used to make walls or cupboards. Some fiberboard has a veneer of wood glued onto the surface to make it look like real wood.

Long-edge pieces of ply are cut and sorted in a Brazilian factory.

Made from Wood

Cellulose fibers from wood can make a variety of materials. The most common and important is paper, and today one in ten of the world's trees is grown for paper. Manufacturers also produce a man-made fiber from cellulose, which is used for weaving textiles and clothes.

Wood contains resins and oils which go into inks, perfumes, soaps, and many other products. Various trees produce their own special products. Pine trees can produce **turpentine**. And several kinds of tropical trees produce a sappy substance called latex, from which we make rubber.

A worker checks a large roll of paper at the end of the papermaking process.

Making Paper

Most paper is made from softwood trees grown specially for the purpose. At a pulp mill, a machine grinds down softwood logs into wood chips. A chemical dissolves the chips to form a soupy pulp, which then goes to a paper mill. There, the pulp is turned into paper on long machines with many rollers. The papermaking machine mixes pulp and water and spreads it out on a wire mesh, then drains, heats, and dries it. This produces large rolls of paper.

Artificial Silk

During the 1880s, scientists used cellulose from wood to create the first man-made fiber. They heated a mixture of natural fibers with chemicals. Then they forced

This photo from the 1940s shows a worker checking spools of rayon in a factory in North Carolina.

the hot, runny resin through tiny holes in a device called a spinneret. This made flexible strands that could be wound onto spools. The inventors called the new substance artificial silk, because they hoped it would replace the expensive silk used to make women's clothing. It was also called viscose, and in 1924 the name was changed to rayon. The fabric became very popular and is still produced today for clothes and furnishings.

Oil from Trees

Artists use an oil called turpentine to thin paints. Turpentine also removes stains from fabric and is an ingredient in some **disinfectants**, **insecticides**, and medicines. Its name comes from terebinth, a small Mediterranean tree. Today, the oil comes mainly from pine trees, and from wood as

it is turned into papermaking pulp. The pulp is heated to give off a **vapor**, which cools to produce turpentine.

RECYCLE RECYCLE RECYCLE RECYCLE

RECYCLED PAPER

Paper is one of the easiest materials to recycle. People put old newspapers and other paper into recycling bins. The used paper is cleaned, and chemicals remove the ink. Then it can be turned back into pulp, ready to be used or mixed with fresh wood pulp and turned into recycled paper.

Burning Wood for Energy

These African children have collected firewood for their families.

Scientists call all plant and animal matter "biomass." Wood forms an important part of the world's biomass. We know that people have burned wood for hundreds of thousands of years for heating and cooking.

More recently, we have learned how to use wood and other plant matter as an energy source to power machines and produce electricity. This is called biomass power.

Fuel for Fires

More than half the wood used in the world every year is burned as fuel. In many African and Asian countries, fuelwood is the people's main source of energy. Together, the two continents produce nearly three-quarters of the world's fuelwood.

In some **developing countries**, people walk many miles (km) every day to collect wood. India is the world's top producer of wood fuel, and more than three-quarters of the wood is used for cooking. Only a small part of the wood comes from managed forests, which adds to the problem of deforestation.

A harvesting machine gathers young willow trees at a plantation in England.

Top Fuelwood Growers

Country	Million cords	Million cubic meters
India	85	307
China	55	200
Brazil	39	140
Ethiopia	27	97
Congo (Dem Rep)	20	73

Source: Food and Agriculture Organization, 2007

Crops for Energy

Trees such as poplar and willow grow very quickly. They can be cut down nearly to ground level then will grow again, so farmers can harvest wood regularly. The farmers cut down poplar and willow **plantations** every two years. Every 2.5 acres (1 ha) produces up to 99 tons (90 t) of wood to be used as biomass fuel or ground into chips for paper or particleboard.

Making Electricity

Wood chips, sawdust, and tree bark can all fuel electric power plants. The wood burns in a **furnace**, which boils water to produce steam. This turns the blades of a **turbine**, which drives a **generator** that produces electricity. Worldwide, some power plants now burn biomass instead of coal.

FROM SOLID TO GAS OR LIQUID

Solid wood can be turned into a gas by a process called gasification. First, a machine called a reactor heats the wood to a very high temperature without much oxygen. It gives off a mixture of gases, including hydrogen and methane, which can drive an electric generator. Another way to convert wood is to use chemicals which break down wood such as poplar to produce a liquid called ethanol. This can be used as a biofuel to replace gasoline and drive cars and trucks.

Working with Wood

Woodworking is one of our oldest crafts. Ancient Egyptian craftsmen made elegant wooden tables, chairs, beds, and chests, as well as their famous coffins (see page 22). About 2,500 years ago, the ancient Chinese also took up woodworking. Today, this is still an important industry around the world.

Woodworkers carve, saw, trim, and join wood to build houses, boats, furniture, and many other items. Carpenters make and repair small wooden objects and larger structures. Joiners make the wooden parts of a building, such as stairs, doors, and window frames. Cabinetmakers make high-quality furniture. Many people also enjoy woodworking as a hobby.

Timber Houses

Wooden houses are traditional in many parts of the world, especially near the vast forests of the northern regions. Log cabins built in Canada and Scandinavia are typical. In other places, wood is used in houses which are also made of brick, stone, or concrete. Some have a wooden framework. Floors may be made from wooden boards or covered with wooden blocks or tiles, called parquet flooring.

Many kinds of houses are built on a wooden framework.

Woodworking Tools

Do-it-yourself woodworkers and professional carpenters use special tools. Woodworkers traditionally use hand tools, but today many are power driven. A woodworker needs different kinds of saws, such as a strong **tenon** saw for precise work and a more delicate coping saw for cutting curves and other shapes. A chisel has a sharp cutting edge for shaving wood. Drills and augers bore holes. Various planes and files smooth the surface of wood.

Joining Pieces of Wood

Woodworkers use joints to fit pieces of wood together. They may also use glue. These joints can make wooden furniture look more attractive. In a dovetail joint, a series of angled tenons fit together. A lap joint is made by overlapping pieces of wood.

In a **mortise** and tenon joint, the mortise is a hole or slot into which a tenon (or projecting piece) fits.

Dovetail joints are often used in boxes and frames. Lap joints are usually glued, nailed, or screwed. The mortise and tenon joint is used for door frames.

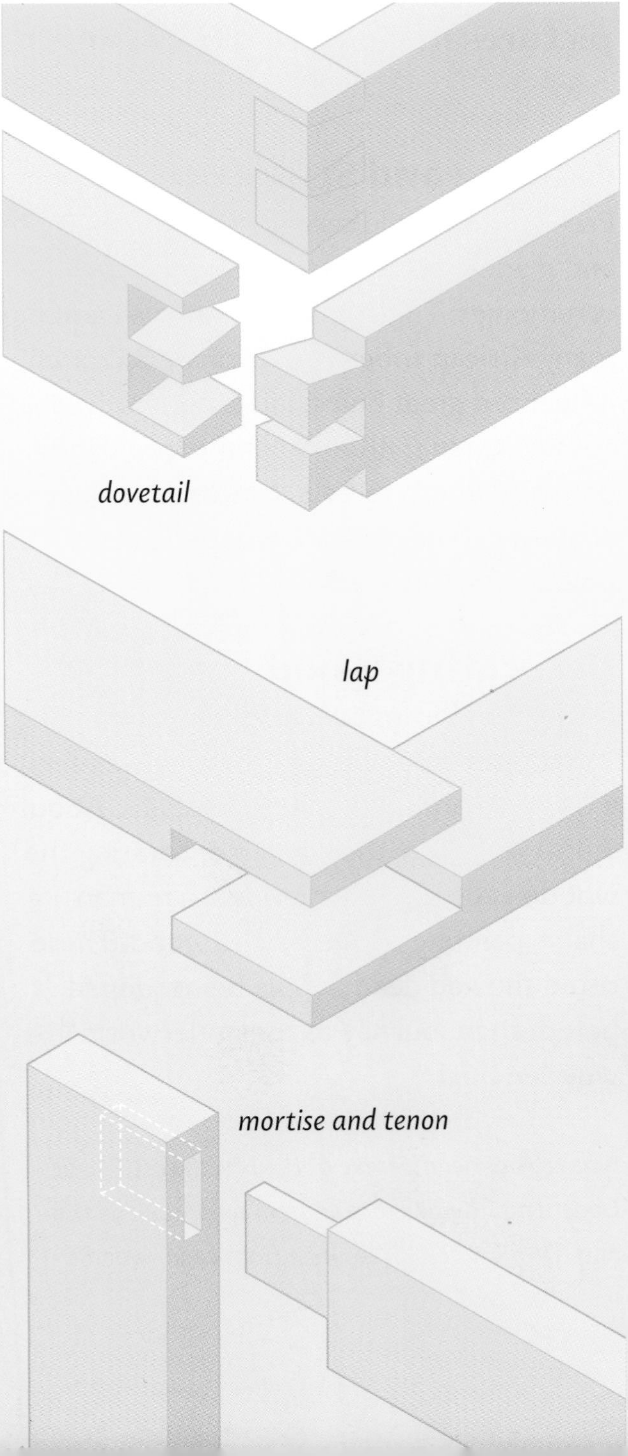

dovetail

lap

mortise and tenon

Making Pictures and Designs

Artists have carved wood since they began using stone and metal tools thousands of years ago. They later painted on wood and then learned to put small layers of wood together to make designs. Artists use the different colors and grains of wood, as well as knots and individual patterns. They also carve pictures in wood to use as prints.

Carving and Sculpture

Prehistoric people carved wooden figurines and made wooden masks to wear at ceremonies. This tradition continues among many African tribes, and their wood carving influenced great European artists such as Pablo Picasso (1881–1973). Among tribes of the northern forests, Native American artisans carved intricate wooden totem poles, as well as masks.

Decorating Wood

Native Americans painted their totem poles with bright colors. Wood painting was also a tradition among ancient Egyptians. About 3,000 years ago, they began decorating the wooden coffins they carved in a human shape, painting scenes on the wood. These often showed dead people being judged before their journey to the underworld in a wooden boat.

Native American people of the Northwest Pacific Coast traditionally make totem poles such as this one. They usually carve them from cedar wood.

Designer Anita Lear Sancha, surrounded by veneers, as she shows a table top she made by marquetry.

Patterns of Veneer

Craftpersons in sixteenth-century Flanders (modern Belgium) invented a new way of using wood to make beautiful designs and pictures. They took thin layers of different kinds of wood, called veneers, and fitted shapes together like a jigsaw puzzle to make a picture. This is called "marquetry." It became popular in neighboring France, where cabinetmakers began using the technique to decorate their furniture. They used different colored woods, ranging from white boxwood all the way to black ebony.

Woodcuts

Wood can also be used to print pictures. The process and the picture are both called woodcuts. The ancient Chinese were probably the first to do this. An artist takes a block of wood and cuts away the parts he does not want to appear in the finished print. This leaves a raised picture on the wood. The artist then rolls ink onto the design and presses the block onto paper. The design is printed in ink on paper.

One of the greatest woodcutters was the German artist Albrecht Dürer (1471–1528). He was followed by many Japanese woodcut artists in the seventeenth century, and their work is still famous today.

The World's Forests Today

Forests cover nearly one-third of the world's land. So there is more than 1.2 acres (0.5 ha) of forest for every person on Earth. However, in the first decade of this century, forests have shrunk by two percent every year. That might not sound like much, but it means that less and less wood is available as each year passes.

There are forests on all the world's continents, except for Antarctica in the extreme south.

Useful Forests

Some forests provide much more useful wood than others. The United Nations' Food and Agriculture Organization (FAO) says that just over one-third of the world's forests are "productive." The top five countries with productive forest plantations are China, the United States, Russia, Brazil, and Sudan.

Trees in Danger

Just as there are many endangered species of animals in the world, many kinds of trees are also in danger of dying out. They include many tropical trees from the rain forests of South America, Africa, and Asia, such as the King William and Parana pine, mahogany, satinwood, teak, and walnut.

RENEWABLE RESOURCE

Trees are a renewable resource, so long as forests are properly managed. That means planting new trees all the time and not cutting down too many trees at one time. The international Forest Stewardship Council (FSC) puts its logo on products (including paper) that are made from trees in well-managed forests. The FSC controls more than 269 million acres (109 million ha) of forest around the world, but this is less than one-tenth of the total.

Where Do Trees Grow?

The only areas where trees don't grow are:
• in the polar regions, where it is too cold;
• in deserts, where it is too dry; and
• in areas where a lot of people live, who cut down the trees and do not plant new ones.

Much of the world's softwood (see page 11) grows in enormous forests across the north of Asia, North America, and Europe. Many hardwoods grow in mild regions above and below the **tropics**. **Tropical rain forests** have the most varied trees, mostly broad-leaved evergreens. Deforestation is a particular problem in rain forests, where environmental organizations are trying to protect our rain forests and stop the clearing of trees.

Ovens turn wood into charcoal in this area of cleared rain forest in northern Brazil.

Recycling Wood

Wood can be recycled in many different ways. Timbers from old buildings can be reused in new ones. Unusable, old wood is ground down into wood chips to make biomass fuel, or to make particleboard or pulp for paper. Recently, environmental groups such as Greenpeace and Friends of the Earth have tried to persuade everyone to use more recycled materials, including wood.

New Life for Old Timber

When an old building is demolished or renovated, workers can carefully take out the timber. They sell it to timber merchants, who treat the wood and then resell it. First, they scan the wood with a metal detector and remove all nails, screws, or other metal pieces. Then they saw it down to a new size, cutting away any pieces or edges that are damaged or rotten. The recycled timber can make new floors, beams, or outside decking.

Choosing and Using Wood

Friends of the Earth suggest that this is the way we should all choose wood.

- Repair, restore, or adapt something you already have that is made of wood. This costs less than buying or making something new and is far better for the world's forests.

A wood-chip mountain in southern Chile. The chips are loaded onto barges and trucks to go to factories.

RECYCLE RECYCLE RECYCLE RECYCLE

- Buy secondhand, recycled, reclaimed, or waste timber. This is a better choice than buying new wood.
- Buy locally produced timber products approved by the Forest Stewardship Council (FSC) (see page 25).

New Paper for Old

Paper (made from wood) is one of the easiest materials to recycle. About 43 percent of the world's paper is recycled, and this figure is increasing. You can take waste newspapers, magazines, and other paper to a recycling center. Many local authorities collect paper for recycling.

Recycled wastepaper often includes several different types made from various fibers, for example, office wastepaper, newsprint, and cardboard. These are usually sorted before being turned back into pulp. The pulp can then be used to make paper of the same or

RECYCLED AT SOURCE

One wood product renews itself on the tree. This is cork, which comes from trees called cork oaks. They grow in Portugal, Spain, and Italy. Their thick, light outer bark makes the natural cork that we use as bottle stoppers, especially for wine. Cork is also used for floors, mats, and other items. Cork strippers cut the bark from a tree every nine years. This does not harm the tree, and the bark regrows until it is ready to be harvested again nine years later. Many wine bottles today have plastic or metal stoppers, which have harmed the cork industry. Cork-oak farmers are struggling to survive.

lower quality than the original paper. It cannot be used to make higher quality paper, unless it is mixed with new pulp.

Wood in the Future

We will need more and more wood in the future, for building houses and making furniture and paper. Wood is likely to become even more important to us as a source of renewable energy. Most people like the look and feel of wood, but perhaps we have more to learn about the ways in which we can use wood.

Labeled teak logs in a timber yard in southern India. Teak is a valuable tropical-hardwood tree.

Learning from Wood

There may be a lot more that botanists and other scientists can learn about wood. At the Royal Institute of Technology in Stockholm, Sweden, researchers are working on a project called Biomime. They are studying wood fibers and cell walls, to see whether we can imitate nature and make new wood-like materials. These could be similar to rayon (see page 17) and might lead to new artificial fibers.

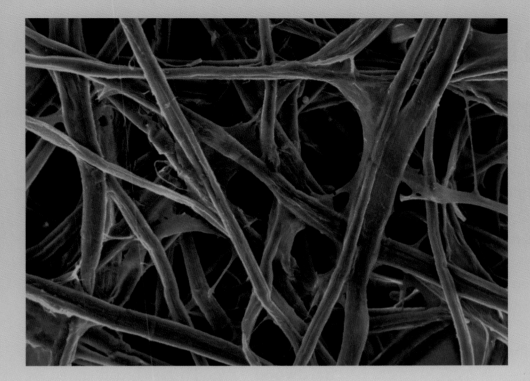

These threadlike cellulose fibers have been magnified 140 times by a microscope. Nanotechnology might make it possible to combine the fibers with other materials.

Changing the Nature of Wood

An alternative to imitating wood is to try to change it. Scientists already know how to alter plants and animals by modifying, or changing, their genes. We all have biological sets of instructions within our cells. These coded instructions are carried by genes, which pass on the code to the next generation. So scientists could change the qualities of wood. They could make some wood harder or grainier, for example. This process is called **genetic modification (GM)**. Many environmentalists say that GM crops are unnatural and could be dangerous to the environment and human health.

Wood on a Tiny Scale

More future changes might come from **nanotechnology**, which uses materials in tiny sizes. Researchers in Canada are using this technology to take tiny particles of cellulose in wood and combine them with other materials. The particles are just 20 nanometers (billionths of a meter) long. Scientists want to combine them with particles of other materials, such as plastics or metals, to make new substances. These could be strong but light, and useful in aircraft, spacecraft, and other vehicles.

Future Forests

More and more forests will be specially planted and managed in the future. People in the forestry industry will want to plant forests of a small number of tree species, because these are easier to grow and control. They will grow trees especially for building, furniture, or paper pulp. Environmentalists want to protect the world's wide range of trees. Many once grew in mixed forests, which are not so useful for wood as a material.

Glossary

biomass fuel   A substance produced from plant or animal matter that provides power; also called biofuel.

blockboard   A block of wood strips with thin sheets of wood glued on.

carbon dioxide (CO_2)   A greenhouse gas given off when fossil fuels (such as coal, oil, or gas) are burned.

cedar   An evergreen cone-bearing tree.

cellulose   A substance that makes up the cell walls of plants.

charcoal   A black form of carbon made by heating wood.

cord   A stack of wood 4 feet (1.2 m) high by 4 feet (1.2 m) wide by 8 feet (2.4 m) long, with a volume of 128 cubic feet (3.6 m³).

deciduous   Describes a tree that sheds its leaves in autumn.

defect   A fault or blemish.

deforestation   Cutting down trees and removing forests.

developing countries   Poorer parts of the world where industry and technology are not advanced.

disinfectant   A substance that destroys tiny organisms that cause disease.

engineered wood   Wood pieces joined together, for example, plywood.

evergreen   Describes a tree that keeps its leaves or needles all year.

fiberboard   A wooden material made by pressing wood fibers into sheets.

flammable   Describes something that can easily catch fire.

flint   A hard gray-black rock.

furnace   An oven-like container for heating materials to very high temperatures.

galley   A large ship with oars and sails.

generator   A machine that turns mechanical energy into electrical energy.

genetic modification   Using technology to change the genes of plants or animals and alter their characteristics.

grain   Wood grain is the pattern made by the way fibers join together to make lines.

greenwood   Newly cut wood.

hardwood   Wood from a broad-leaved, deciduous tree, such as an oak.

heartwood   The dark, older wood at the center of a tree trunk.

hydrant   A water pipe in the street that firefighters can use.

insecticide   A chemical that kills insects.

lignin   A substance that holds plant fibers together and makes plants rigid and woody.

mortise   A hole or slot cut into wood; a tenon fits into it to make a joint.

nanotechnology   Technology that uses materials in tiny, microscopic sizes.

particleboard   Wooden sheets made by pressing wood chips and sawdust together.

photosynthesis   The process plants use to make food from carbon dioxide and water.

plantation   A large group of trees planted in one area.

plow   A heavy farming tool that breaks up soil.

plywood   Boards made by pressing and gluing together thin layers of wood.

pollution   Damage to the environment caused by harmful substances.

prehistoric   Describes the time before people recorded history in writing.

raw material   A natural material, such as wood, before it is processed and used.

resin   A sticky substance produced by some plants.

sapwood   The light, softer wood between a tree's bark and heartwood.

sod   Soil with grass growing on it.

softwood   Wood from a needle-leaved evergreen tree, such as a pine.

tenon   A projecting piece of wood that fits into a mortise to form a joint.

tropical rain forest   Thick evergreen forest in tropical areas with heavy rainfall.

tropics   The world's warmest regions just above and below the equator (the imaginary line around the middle of the Earth).

turbine   A machine with rotating blades that turn a shaft.

turpentine   An oil that comes mainly from pine trees.

vapor   A moist gas.

veneer   A thin layer of wood attached to another material.

xylem   A scientific word for plant tissue or wood.

Web Sites

Information on the International Forest Stewardship Council (see page 24) and its work managing the world's forests.
www.fsc.org

National Geographic web site discusses deforestation and global warming.
http://environment.nationalgeographic.com/environment/global-warming/deforestation-overview.html

How lumber is made.
http://www.madehow.com/Volume-3/Lumber.html

How various U.S. cities use wood.
http://www.na.fs.fed.us/spfo/pubs/misc/utilizingmunitrees/index.htm

Fascinating facts about cork and how it is produced.
www.corkfacts.com/natlcrk11.htm

Index